The Adventures of Scuba Jack
Copyright 2021 by Beth Costanzo
All rights reserved

Our oceans, rivers, and other bodies of water are home to some of the most awesome looking creatures. Lots of our attention is focused on creatures on land or in the sky, but our waters are home to many fascinating creatures that don't look like anything we normally see.

www.adventuresofscubajack.com

As an example of this, we only need to look at **sea stars**. Also called *starfish*, sea stars are found on the seabeds of our world's ocean. They have their signature look and are fascinating to look at. Whether you want to learn more about a **sea star** you have recently seen or are simply curious about this creature, join me as we explore what makes the **sea star** so special.

www.adventuresofscubajack.com

Some Captivating Facts About Sea Stars

www.adventuresofscubajack.com

Whenever you look at or are talking about the **sea star**, one of the first things that you will notice is its *appearance*. **Sea stars** are marine invertebrates. Often, they have a central disc and five arms extending from that disc. But having said this, some species of **sea stars** can have more arms. Some species have six or seven arms while other species of **sea stars** have 10 to 15 arms. The arms are in a species called the Antarctic Labidiaster annulatus, which can have over 50 arms.

www.adventuresofscubajack.com

Beyond all of these arms, **sea stars** are often brightly colored. Some of the most well-known sea stars are in different shades of orange or red. However, you can find other **sea stars** that are grey, brown, or even blue. There are about 1,500 living species of **sea stars** today. These **sea stars** have some key differences, but all of them look fairly close to the **sea stars** that you have seen in books, movies, or television shows.

www.adventuresofscubajack.com

Some of the earliest **sea stars** were found around *450 million years* ago. That said, finding the fossils for these ancient **sea stars** is very difficult because **sea stars** disintegrate after they die. Adding to the difficulty is that two major extinction events occurred hundreds of millions of years ago, which prevents us from learning more about these ancient **sea stars**. Today, the lifespan of **sea stars** depends on the particular species. Some **sea star** species can live for about five years while others live for approximately ten years. The maximum recorded lifespan for some **sea stars** is *34 years*.

www.adventuresofscubajack.com

Now, let's talk about where you can find **sea stars**. Because **sea stars** have a delicate balance of minerals called *electrolytes*, they cannot live in fresh water. Instead, you can find **sea stars** in all of the world's oceans. Some of the habitats where **sea stars** are found include *tropical coral reefs, seagrass meadows*, tidal pools, and even down 20,000 feet to the deep sea floor. Coastal areas have the most diversity of **sea star** species.

www.adventuresofscubajack.com

Some of the earliest **sea stars** were found around *450 million years* ago. That said, finding the fossils for these ancient **sea stars** is very difficult because **sea stars** disintegrate after they die. Adding to the difficulty is that two major extinction events occurred hundreds of millions of years ago, which prevents us from learning more about these ancient **sea stars**. Today, the lifespan of **sea stars** depends on the particular species. Some **sea star** species can live for about five years while others live for approximately ten years. The maximum recorded lifespan for some **sea stars** is *34 years*.

www.adventuresofscubajack.com

Now, let's talk about where you can find **sea stars**. Because **sea stars** have a delicate balance of minerals called *electrolytes*, they cannot live in fresh water. Instead, you can find **sea stars** in all of the world's oceans. Some of the habitats where **sea stars** are found include *tropical coral reefs, seagrass meadows*, tidal pools, and even down 20,000 feet to the deep sea floor. Coastal areas have the most diversity of **sea star** species.

www.adventuresofscubajack.com

Sea stars, like all other ocean creatures, need to eat. They eat all kinds of marine life, including sponges, snails, microalgae, and bivalves. Several **sea star** species can even absorb organic materials from the surrounding water. The actual process of capturing and feeding prey depends on the species of **sea stars**. For example, one **sea star** called the Pisaster brevispinus captures prey by using some specialized tube feet to dig into animals like clams.

www.adventuresofscubajack.com

Like other sea creatures, **sea stars** are hunted by other animals. Some of the most common predators of **sea stars** include conspecifics, sea anemones, crabs, gulls, sea otters, and other fish. To protect themselves from these predators, **sea stars** have substances in their body walls that have unpleasant flavors. Some other **sea star** species have toxins in their body that can protect them if they are being hunted.

www.adventuresofscubajack.com

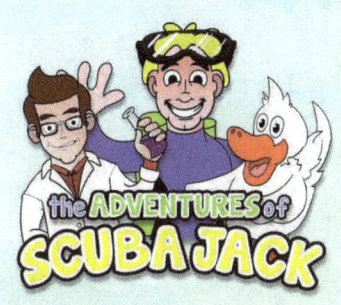

Most species of **sea stars** have separate male and female individuals. To have children, the male and female **sea stars** mate. But having said this, some species of **sea stars** are *asexual*, meaning that they can have children without a partner.

www.adventuresofscubajack.com

One of the coolest things about **sea stars** is that they can grow back lost arms. In fact, with enough time, they can even regrow an entirely new limb. **Sea stars** may lose these body parts if it is detached by a predator or actively shed by the **sea star** if it is escaping a predator. Regrowing these lost arms or limbs can take several months or years. As they are regrowing these body parts, however, sea stars are at risk of infections. This means that if they get sick, sea stars can die as they are growing back their arms or limbs.

www.adventuresofscubajack.com

Finally, **sea stars** are extremely important to the health of their marine communities. This is because of their relatively large size, diets that encompass a wide range of things, and its ability to quickly adapt to different environments. That said, they aren't perfect. **Sea stars** have sometimes caused some negative effects on their ecosystems. Specifically, some **sea stars** of the crown-of-thorns species have damaged coral reefs near northeast Australia. Coral cover declined, which affected other fish who feed on reefs.

www.adventuresofscubajack.com

Some Other Fun Facts About the Sea Star

As you can tell, the sea star is a creature that plays a big role in our world's oceans. Not only is it cool to look at, but the sea star is a key animal in many habits. Along with the facts above, here are some more fun facts about the sea star.

www.adventuresofscubajack.com

The crown-of-thorns sea star isn't attractive to many predators because it contains sharp spines that have toxins and bright warning colors.

Sea stars can expel foreign objects from their bodies. While this can be helpful for many different purposes, it makes it difficult for researchers to attach tags to track them.

www.adventuresofscubajack.com

Sea stars are sometimes eaten in Japan, China, and Micronesia.

Sea stars can be taken from their habitat and sold to tourists in many different countries.

Sea stars do not have a brain or blood.

Sea stars can move by using hundreds of tube feet.

 Sea stars technically aren't fish. Unlike fish, they do not have scales, fins, or gills.

 Sea stars have an eye spot at the end of each arm.

www.adventuresofscubajack.com

Sea Stars Activities

www.adventuresofscubajack.com

SEA STARS
WHAT DO YOU KNOW?

1. Sea stars have five _____.
2. Sea stars eat _____ by forcing their cardiac stomach between their shells.
3. Sea stars are sometimes called _____.
4. Sea stars are _____. This means that they do not have spines.
5. If a sea star loses an arm, it can grow a new one. This is called _____.
6. Sea stars have two _____.
7. Sea stars have tiny _____ at the end of each arm
8. Sea stars bring water into their bodies through the _____.
9. Sea stars move slowly using their _____.
10. Sea stars do not have _____.

regeneration - starfish - madreporite - tube feet - brains - invertebrates - arms - shellfish - eyes - stomachs

SEA STAR MAZE

Circle the correct number

2   3   4   5

2   3   4   5

2   3   4   5

2   3   1   5

TEXTURED SEA STAR

- To make a textures sea star, cut out is sea star shape from thick paper like cardstock.
- Paint the sea star your favorite color.
- Before the paint dries, sprinkle on the project to add texture.
- An alternative would be to coat the sea star with glue. Next sprinkle rice or mini pasta stars that have been dyed with food coloring over the sea star.

Please visit

www.adventuresofscubajack.com

And Click on the "Read To Me" section.

Download our Awesome Sea Star Booklet

And try your Expertise on our

Super Fun Sea Star Quiz!

www.ingramcontent.com/pod-product-compliance
Lightning Source LLC
Chambersburg PA
CBHW060429010526
44118CB00017B/2420